T0020428

Selena Gomez

Mental Health Advocate

by Elizabeth Neuenfeldt

BLASTOFF!
2
READERS

BELLWETHER MEDIA • MINNEAPOLIS, MN

Blastoff! Readers are carefully developed by literacy experts to build reading stamina and move students toward fluency by combining standards-based content with developmentally appropriate text.

 Level 1 provides the most support through repetition of high-frequency words, light text, predictable sentence patterns, and strong visual support.

 Level 2 offers early readers a bit more challenge through varied sentences, increased text load, and text-supportive special features.

 Level 3 advances early-fluent readers toward fluency through increased text load, less reliance on photos, advancing concepts, longer sentences, and more complex special features.

★ **Blastoff! Universe**

Reading Level

Grade
K

Grades
1–3

Grade
4

This edition first published in 2022 by Bellwether Media, Inc.

No part of this publication may be reproduced in whole or in part without written permission of the publisher. For information regarding permission, write to Bellwether Media, Inc., Attention: Permissions Department, 6012 Blue Circle Drive, Minnetonka, MN 55343.

Library of Congress Cataloging-in-Publication Data

LC record for Selena Gomez: Mental Health Advocate available at: https://lccn.loc.gov/2021041240

Editor: Betsy Rathburn   Designer: Gabriel Hilger

Printed in the United States of America, North Mankato, MN.

Table of Contents

Who Is Selena Gomez?   4

Getting Her Start   8

Changing the World   12

Selena's Future   18

Glossary   22

To Learn More   23

Index   24

Who Is Selena Gomez?

Selena Gomez is a singer and actor.

Selena is also an **advocate**! She speaks out about **mental health**.

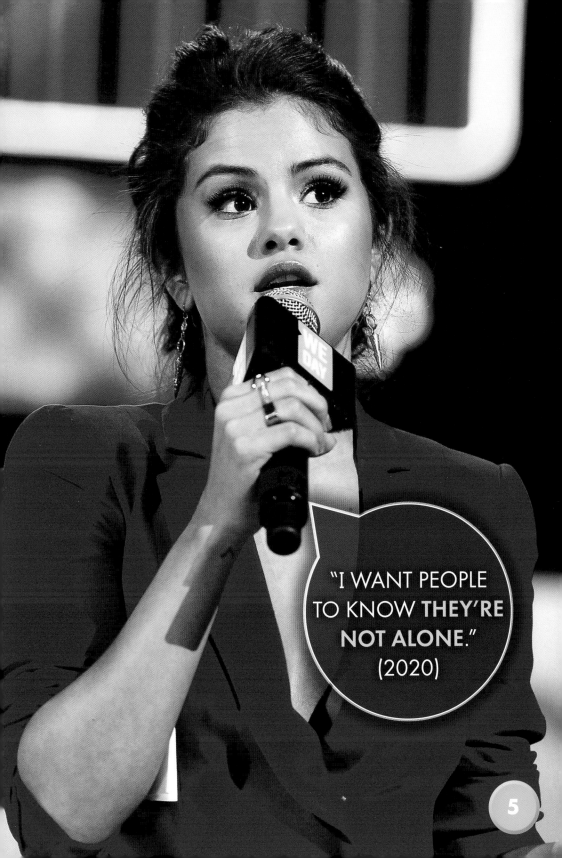

"I WANT PEOPLE TO KNOW THEY'RE NOT ALONE." (2020)

Selena was born on July 22, 1992. She grew up in Texas.

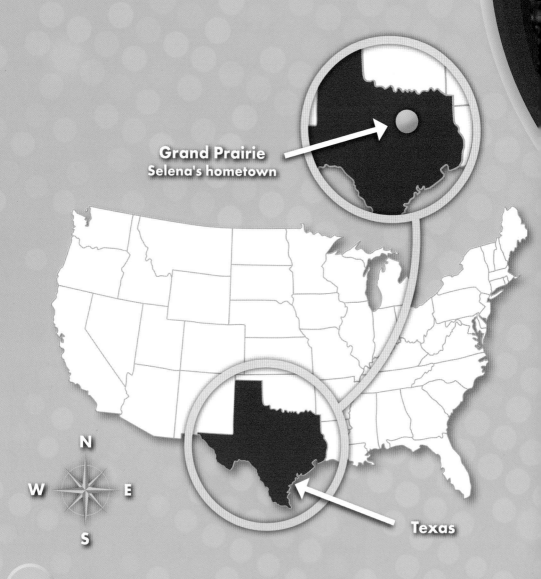

Grand Prairie
Selena's hometown

N
W E
S

Texas

Selena with her
mom, Mandy

Selena's mom was an actor.
Selena wanted to be an
actor, too!

Getting Her Start

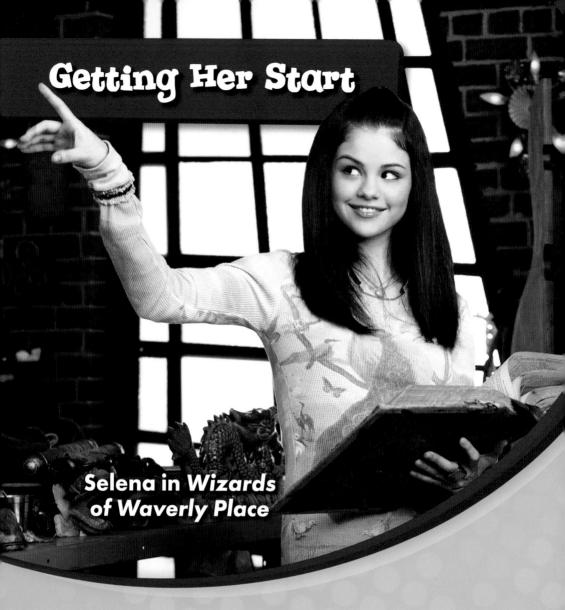

Selena in *Wizards of Waverly Place*

Selena began acting in 2002. She was on the show *Barney & Friends*.

In 2007, she starred in *Wizards of Waverly Place.* Many kids watched the show!

Selena Gomez Profile

Birthday: July 22, 1992

Hometown: Grand Prairie, Texas

Field: music, acting, mental health advocacy

Schooling: high school

Influences:
- Mandy Teefey (mother)
- Taylor Swift (singer)

Selena quickly became popular. She was in more movies and shows. She also made music.

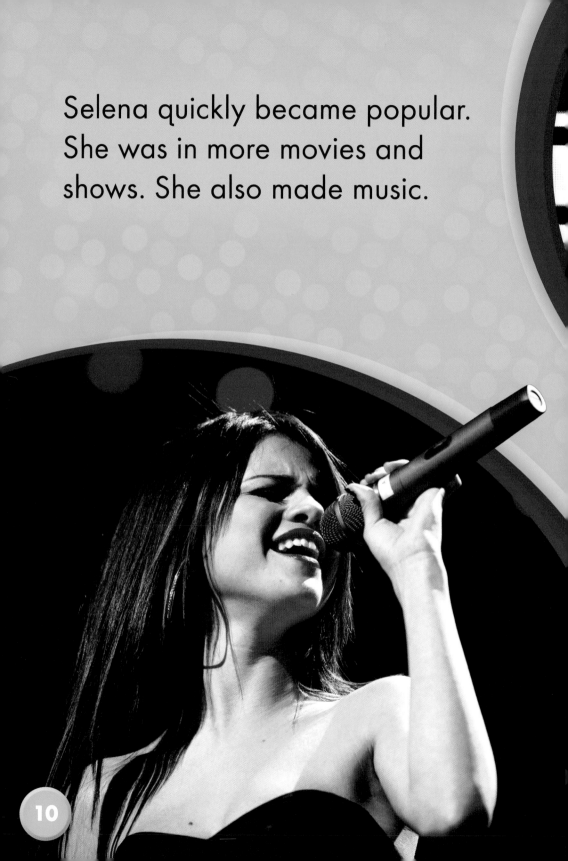

Selena accepting an award at the 2016 American Music Awards

Selena won many **awards**!

Changing the World

In 2015, Selena shared that she has **lupus**. It affects her **physical** health.

It also affects her mental health. She battles **anxiety** and **depression**.

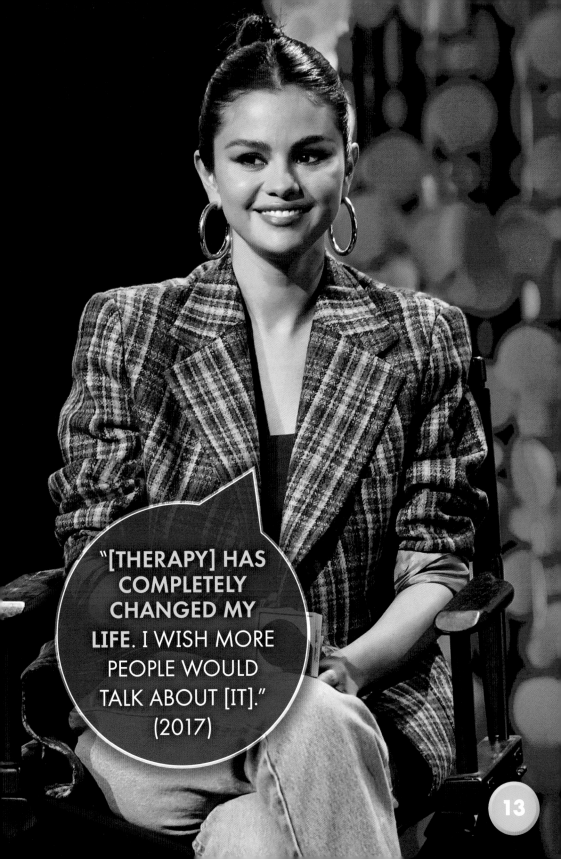

"[THERAPY] HAS COMPLETELY CHANGED MY LIFE. I WISH MORE PEOPLE WOULD TALK ABOUT [IT]." (2017)

But Selena stays strong! She speaks out for mental health. She talks about the benefits of **therapy**.

She has also raised money for lupus research.

Selena Gomez Timeline

2007	Selena stars in *Wizards of Waverly Place*
2009	Selena wins her first of many Teen Choice Awards
2019	Selena wins the 2019 McLean Award for Mental Health Advocacy
JULY 2020	Selena starts the Rare Impact Fund and plans to raise $100 million dollars in 10 years
OCTOBER 2020	Selena wins the Arts Award at the 33rd Hispanic Heritage Awards
2021	Selena forms Mental Health 101 to help kids learn about mental health

Selena won awards for speaking out.

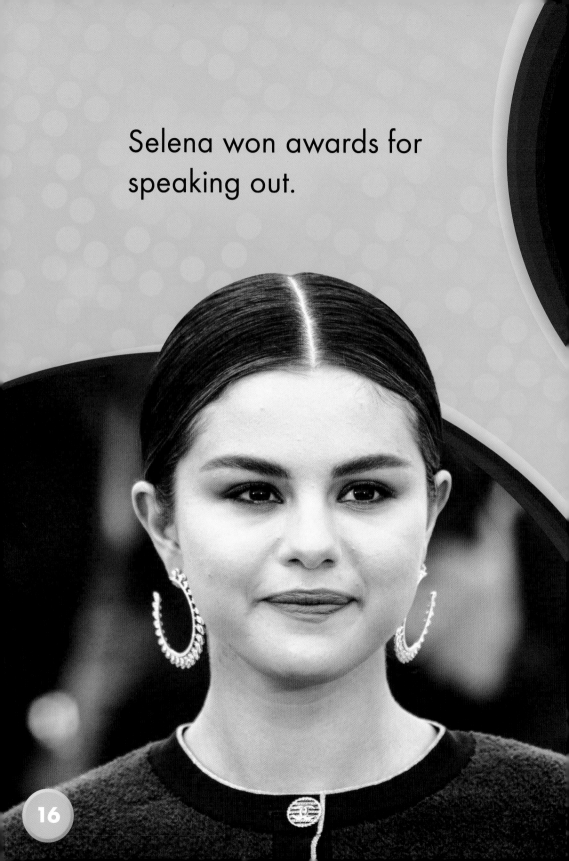

In 2020, she formed a **fund**. She wants to make therapy more **accessible**.

Selena's Future

Selena still sings and acts. She makes music in Spanish and English!

Selena is a **producer**, too.
She works on movies and shows.

Selena promoting a
TV show she produced

19

In 2021, Selena started Mental Health 101. It helps kids learn about mental health.

She wants kids to know that their mental health matters!

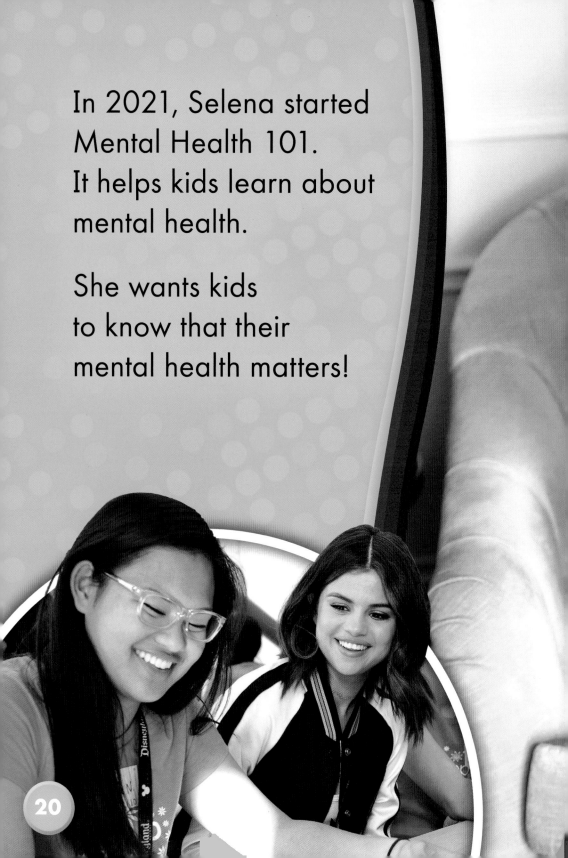

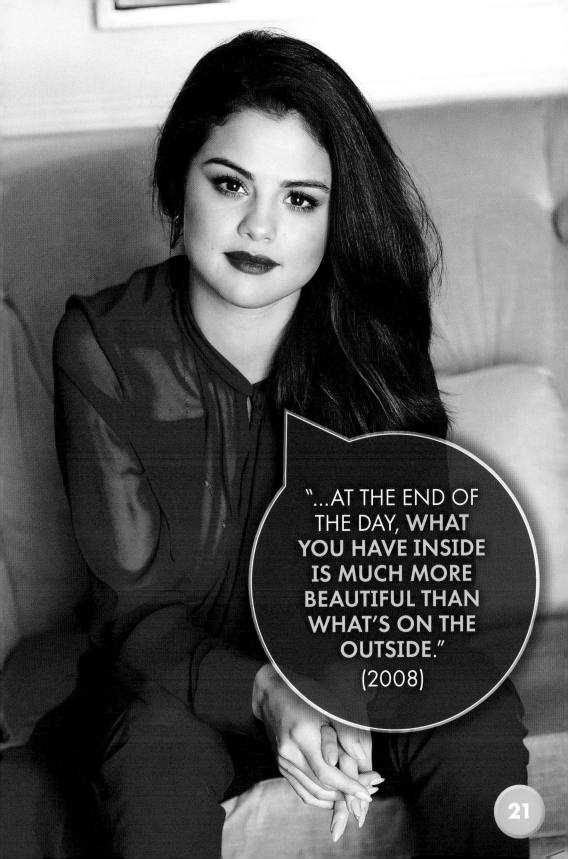

"...AT THE END OF THE DAY, WHAT YOU HAVE INSIDE IS MUCH MORE BEAUTIFUL THAN WHAT'S ON THE OUTSIDE." (2008)

Glossary

accessible—able to be used

advocate—a person who supports and argues for a cause

anxiety—a condition in which a person experiences fear or nervousness about what might happen

awards—rewards or prizes that are given for a job well done

depression—a condition in which a person feels very sad and hopeless

fund—an amount of money that is used for a special purpose

lupus—an illness that affects different parts of the body and cannot be cured

mental health—a person's mental and emotional state

physical—related to the body

producer—a person who takes charge and provides the money to make something

therapy—the treatment for an illness or injury of the body or mind

To Learn More

AT THE LIBRARY

Chang, Kirsten. *Understanding Emotions*. Minneapolis, Minn.: Bellwether Media, 2022.

Lajiness, Katie. *Selena Gomez: Pop Star*. Minneapolis, Minn.: Abdo Publishing, 2018.

Leaf, Christina. *Michelle Obama: Health Advocate*. Minneapolis, Minn.: Bellwether Media, 2019.

ON THE WEB

Factsurfer.com gives you a safe, fun way to find more information.

1. Go to www.factsurfer.com.

2. Enter "Selena Gomez" into the search box and click 🔍.

3. Select your book cover to see a list of related content.

Index

actor, 4, 7, 8, 18

advocate, 4

anxiety, 12

awards, 11, 16

Barney & Friends, 8

depression, 12

fund, 17

kids, 9, 20

lupus, 12, 15

mental health, 4, 12, 14, 20

Mental Health 101, 20

mom, 7

movies, 10, 19

music, 10, 18

producer, 19

profile, 9

quotes, 5, 13, 21

shows, 8, 9, 10, 19

singer, 4, 18

Texas, 6

therapy, 14, 17

timeline, 15

Wizards of Waverly Place, 8, 9

The images in this book are reproduced through the courtesy of: Kurt Krieger - Corbis/ Getty Images, front cover (Selena Gomez); Belight, front cover (rocks); Ink Drop, pp. 3, 23; Kevin Winter/ Getty Images, pp. 4 (inset), 12-13; Steve Jennings/ Stringer/ Getty Images, pp. 4-5; Kathy Hutchins, pp. 6-7; Album/ Alamy, pp. 8-9; DFree, p. 9; Bryan Bedder/ Getty Images, pp. 10-11 (bottom); Lester Cohen/ Getty Images, pp. 10-11 (top); Jesse Grant/ Stringer/ Getty Images, pp. 12 (inset), 16-17 (top); Jemal Countess/ Stringer/ Getty Images, pp. 14-15; Allstar Picture Library Ltd/ Alamy, pp. 16-17 (bottom); Emma McIntyre/ AMA2019/ Getty Images, p. 18; Allen Berezovsky/ Getty Images, pp. 18-19; Donato Sardella/ Getty Images, p. 20 (inset); Angela Weiss/ Stringer/ Getty Images, pp. 20-21.